SOUTH CAMPUS

Food Science:
YOU ARE WHAT YOU EAT

SOUTH CAMPUS

LYONS TWP H.S. LIBRARY
WESTERN SPRINGS, ILLINOIS

Nutrition Facts

Serving Size 5 oz. (144g)
Servings Per Container 4

Amount Per Serving

Calories 310   Calories from Fat 100

	% Daily Value
Total Fat 15g	21%
Saturated Fat 2.6g	17%
Trans Fat 1g	
Cholesterol 118mg	39%
Sodium 560mg	
Total Carbohydrate 12g	28%
Dietary Fiber 1g	
Sugars 1g	
Protein 24g	

Vitamin A 1% • Vitamin C 2%
Calcium 2% • Iron 5%

Percent Daily Values are based on a 2,000
diet. Your daily values may be higher or lower
depending on your calorie needs.

Essential Library

An Imprint of Abdo Publishing | www.abdopublishing.com

History of
Science

Food Science:
YOU ARE WHAT YOU EAT

by Amanda Lanser

Content Consultant

Sarah W. Tracy
Associate Professor of Honors and the History of Medicine
University of Oklahoma

Calories from Fat 100

	% Daily Value
Total Fat 15g	21%
Saturated Fat 2.6g	17%
Trans Fat 1g	
Cholesterol 118mg	39%
Sodium 560mg	28%
Total Carbohydrate 12g	4%
Dietary Fiber 1g	
Sugars 1g	
Protein 24g	

Vitamin A 1%	•	Vitamin C 2%
Calcium 2%	•	Iron 5%

*Percent Daily Values are based on a 2,000 calorie diet. Your daily values may be higher or lower depending on your calorie needs.

	Calories	2,000
Total Fat	Less Than	65g
Saturated Fat	Less Than	20g
Cholesterol	Less Than	300mg

History of
Science

www.abdopublishing.com

Published by Abdo Publishing, a division of ABDO, PO Box 398166, Minneapolis, Minnesota 55439. Copyright © 2015 by Abdo Consulting Group, Inc. International copyrights reserved in all countries. No part of this book may be reproduced in any form without written permission from the publisher. Essential Library™ is a trademark and logo of Abdo Publishing.

Printed in the United States of America, North Mankato, Minnesota

102014
012015

Cover Photos: Nixx Photography/Shutterstock Images; Shelby Allison/Shutterstock Images; Shutterstock Images; Sergiy Kuzmin/Shutterstock Images

Interior Photos: Nixx Photography/Shutterstock Images, 1, 3; Shelby Allison/Shutterstock Images, 1, 3, 83; Shutterstock Images, 1, 3, 19, 90; Sergiy Kuzmin/Shutterstock Images, 1, 3; Bettmann/Corbis, 7, 51, 54, 76; Farm Security Administration/Office of War/Library of Congress, 9, 69; Library of Congress, 11; Alex Proimos, 12; Anton Ivanov/Shutterstock Images, 15; Peter Paul Rubens, 17; Tim Ur/Shutterstock Images, 24; Juan Gaertner/Shutterstock Images, 27; World History Archive/Newscom, 29, 39, 43; Brand X Pictures/Thinkstock, 31; Zastolskiy Victor/Shutterstock Images, 33; Markus Mainka/Shutterstock Images, 34; Austrian Archives/Corbis, 41; Public Domain, 45; Everett Collection/Newscom, 49; AP Images, 57, 64; Centers for Disease Control and Prevention, 61; United Kingdom Government, 62; Harris & Ewing Collection/Library of Congress, 67; US Agriculture Department, 71; Digital Vision/Thinkstock, 79; Thanamat Somwan/Shutterstock Images, 87; Elena Shashkina/Shutterstock Images, 89; Ira Bostic/Shutterstock Images, 92; Edward Parsons/EPA/Newscom, 95

Editor: Jenna Gleisner
Series Designer: Craig Hinton

Library of Congress Control Number: 2014943871

Cataloging-in-Publication Data
Lanser, Amanda.
 Food science: you are what you eat / Amanda Lanser.
  p. cm. -- (History of science)
 ISBN 978-1-62403-560-9 (lib. bdg.)
 Includes bibliographical references and index.
 1. Food science--History--Juvenile literature. 2. Nutrition--Juvenile literature. I. Title.
 664--dc23
                                             2014943871

Contents

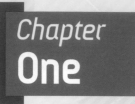

Rickets, Putrid Meat, AND PLUMPY'NUT

$$\frac{a+b}{a} = \frac{a}{b} = 1{,}618$$

In approximately 500 BCE, Greek scholar Herodotus was inspecting the skeletons of soldiers killed in battle a century earlier in the Egyptian town of Pelusium. He noticed the skulls of the Persian soldiers were so thin a small pebble could crush them. The skulls of the Egyptian soldiers, however, were so strong only a large rock caused damage. When Herodotus inquired about the unusual observation, townspeople provided little information. The only difference they could remember was the Persians wore turbans, while the Egyptians fought bareheaded, exposing their heads to the sun. What caused the Persian skulls to crack so easily, while all the Egyptian skulls were strong?

More than 2,000 years later in 1650 CE, Professor Francis Glisson studied at Cambridge University in England. He was investigating a disease affecting many

It wasn't until the 1920s scientists discovered vitamin D—even in the form of artificial sunlight—was necessary to prevent rickets.

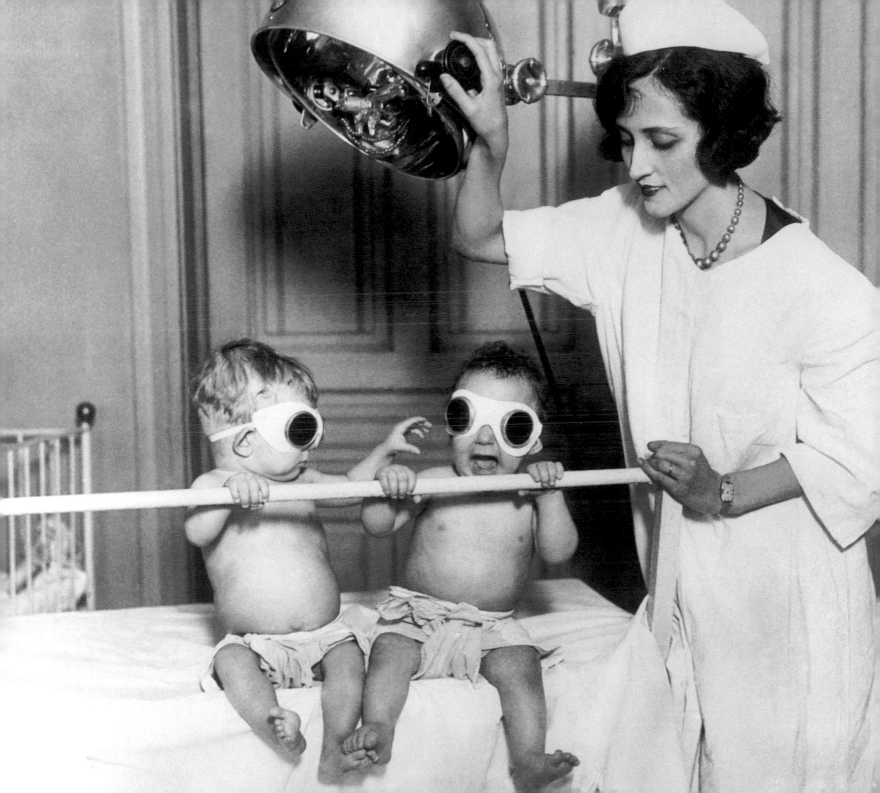

RICKETS ACROSS THE WORLD

Rickets did not only affect children in the impoverished neighborhoods of England's cities. In 1921, rickets affected 75 percent of all infants in New York City.[1] The disease continues to be a problem. Today, children in Africa and parts of tropical Asia suffer from rickets, mainly from a lack of calcium in their diets. Rickets is also becoming common again in wealthier nations, including the United States and European countries. Doctors believe this may be due to children spending more time indoors and not producing enough vitamin D through sunlight or from wearing more sunscreen, which prevents the sun's UV rays from penetrating the skin.

young children and old women. The disease caused weak bones and deformities, including bowed legs, curved spines, square skulls, and poor teeth. It also caused people to suffer from swollen joints and abdomens. Professor Glisson published his account of the disease. However, he was not able to identify the cause of the bone deformities and other symptoms.

For the next 200 years, incidents of the disease came and went, often aligning with the quality of the food crop. Then, the Industrial Revolution transformed English society. People poured into the cities from the countryside to work. They lived in crowded neighborhoods called slums, where the soot from factories blocked the sun's rays. A poor diet of primarily white bread and tea was the only food people were able to afford. The disease outlined by Glisson, now called rickets, was common in poor urban children. In 1890, it was discovered the disease was more common in places where there was less sunlight. Soon, doctors were prescribing time in the sun to prevent rickets. The underlying cause of rickets, however, would not be discovered until the 1920s, when scientists found a link between vitamin D,

Doctors considered rickets, which causes bowed legs, to be the most common childhood disease in the 1920s.

which human bodies produce after receiving sunlight, and bone growth. The bone deformities and weakness caused by rickets were the results of a lack of vitamin D, calcium, or phosphate in a child's diet. Exposure to sunlight and eating dairy and green vegetables containing vitamin D can prevent the disease. It took scientists and physicians nearly 2,500 years to discover the quality of a person's diet could prevent this debilitating disease.

Meatpacking in Manhattan

Rickets was not the only nutritional concern in the 1800s. In 1884, Mathilde Wendt, Mary Trautmann, and roughly a dozen other women living in the Beekman Hill neighborhood of New York City were angry. Various meat industries were fouling the air and streets near their homes. They established the Ladies' Health Protective Association and began conducting their own inspections of offending slaughterhouses.

What they witnessed turned even their strong stomachs. Slaughterhouse floors were covered in dried blood from the slaughtering process. Unusable animal parts rotted while fresh meat was thrown on top of them. The women confronted the slaughterhouse owners about these unsanitary conditions. When owners did not make changes, the women demonstrated outside their facilities and

After the Ladies' Health Protective Association raised awareness of the issue, inspectors began checking meat and conditions in slaughterhouses in the early 1900s.

complained before the city's Board of Health. An 1891 issue of *The Illustrated American* magazine described the women's persistence:

> *In every case the outrage against the public good-health was carefully investigated [by the Ladies' Health Protective Association], and the fact of existing evil . . . was brought before the Board of Health.*[3]

The tireless work of the women in the Ladies' Health Protective Association helped create more sanitary slaughterhouse conditions and improved food safety.

Mothers can give their children Plumpy'Nut in their own homes and do not need to admit their children to hospitals for treatment.

Plumping Kids Up with Plumpy'Nut

More than a century after the Ladies' Health Protective Association conducted its investigations, millions of children worldwide under the age of five suffered from the life-threatening condition severe acute malnutrition (SAM). SAM affects children who do not have access to nutritious food, have severe illnesses affecting their weight, or other conditions. Often, lack of food is due to some type of emergency or poor living conditions, such as those experienced in refugee camps.

Children with SAM have nutritional needs that cannot be met with standard foods. Food scientists created a product to treat SAM called Plumpy'Nut. Plumpy'Nut is a nutritious paste made of milk powder, peanuts, whey, sugar, oil, vitamins, and minerals. In its foil container, it can keep for as long as two years without refrigeration. It is meant to feed children with SAM who are six months of age and older. A child with no other health conditions weighing between 11 and 15 pounds (5 and 7 kg) can recover from SAM by eating two packets of Plumpy'Nut each day for six to eight weeks. A child weighing more than 15 pounds (7 kg) needs three packets. Aid groups distribute Plumpy'Nut to families for free. By improving nutrition and providing groups of people with a consistent source of quality food, Plumpy'Nut is helping eliminate deaths from SAM.

Food Science: Helping Society

Studying the cause of rickets, taking action against the unsanitary condition of slaughterhouses, and developing new food technologies to fight malnutrition are three examples of innovation in food science. In each case, scientists, doctors, and public health advocates worked to improve the nutrition, health, and food security of

READY-TO-USE THERAPEUTIC FOODS

Plumpy'Nut is one example of what international food aid organizations call ready-to-use therapeutic food (RUTF). The first RUTF was developed in the 1990s after a famine killed nearly 125,000 people in Somalia. The foods are very energy and nutrient dense and a child can eat them right out of the packet without adding water. Though RUTF is a lifesaver for children who are already severely malnourished, in some instances the foods are being used to prevent SAM. Some scientists believe this use of the product may come with some negative consequences, including reduction in breastfeeding, which is believed to be the best solution to malnutrition in the long-term for small children.

AVOIDING A FOODBORNE ILLNESS

Food scientists at the University of Maryland have several suggestions for avoiding illnesses from contaminated foods both in homes and in industries, including:

+ washing hands before and after handling food, using the bathroom, or touching animals

+ washing equipment, such as knives and cutting boards, in hot water and soap

+ wearing gloves when preparing and cooking food if hands are cut or have sores

+ cooking meat to recommended temperatures

+ separating meats from other foods, such as vegetables

+ checking labels for use-by dates and avoiding grocery store products with broken seals or from bulging cans[4]

individuals as well as populations of people. The study of food science is tied to the basic human need for safe, high-quality food and access to food sources. Food scientists study the chemical, physical, and biological makeup of foods to make sure they are nutritious, wholesome, cost-effective, and free of harmful contaminants. Food scientists play an active role in keeping the public healthy and safe by helping lawmakers create food laws and policies that make public welfare a priority.

The body of scientific knowledge and food laws on which the world relies today has been gathered throughout hundreds of years. People have studied food quality, safety, and security for thousands of years. They have found the building blocks of a healthy diet include not only fat, protein, and carbohydrates, but also vitamins and minerals. They discovered adding chemicals to alter the color and taste of food can put human health at risk. Food scientists have developed ways to make society's food sources more secure with better growing techniques and innovative storage and preservation technologies, such as refrigeration.

Food scientists continue searching for solutions to world hunger and malnutrition.

Food science is an evolving field. Many challenges still remain, including malnutrition and hunger in war-torn countries and regions affected by severe weather due to climate change. Some scientists will tackle ways to prevent large outbreaks of foodborne illnesses. Others may focus on how the processed convenience foods many people enjoy today may negatively affect their health. Humans have been consuming food for tens of thousands of years, but scientists, doctors, and society still have much to discover about what makes food nutritious, safe, and secure.

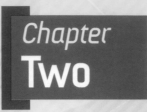
Ancient Theories
TO RENAISSANCE
REVELATIONS

$$\frac{a+b}{a} = \frac{a}{b} = 1,618$$

Though the term *food science* is relatively modern, people have been studying food and the effects it has on the body for thousands of years. Scientists believe humans were making yogurt as a way to preserve dairy foods approximately 4,500 years ago. The study of food became the focus of the work of several prominent thinkers in ancient Greece and Rome as well.

Ancient Greek thinkers were interested in how food was used by the body, how it caused illness, and how to secure the food supply. In 600 BCE, philosopher Alcmaeon was the first person to document the idea that humans required a moderate amount

Hippocrates introduced the thought that humans only needed as much food for energy as they would use.

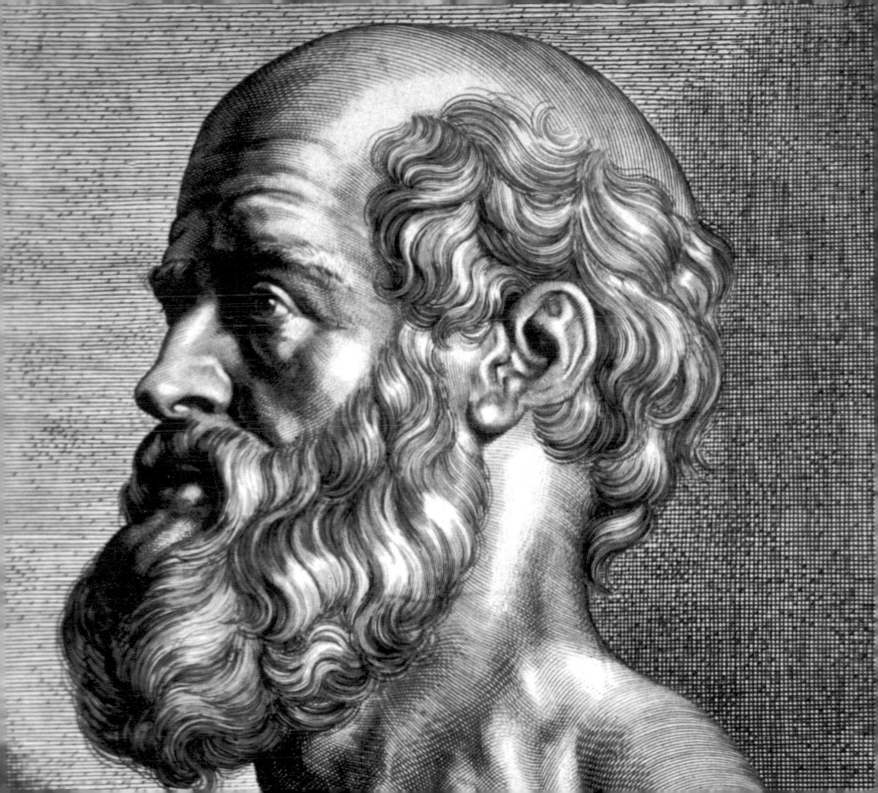

of food to remain healthy. He also claimed eating too much or too little had a negative effect on the body.

In 460 BCE, Greek physician Hippocrates expanded on Alcmaeon's ideas and developed a new way of thinking about food that would linger into the Renaissance. Like Alcmaeon, Hippocrates believed people needed to eat in moderation to remain healthy. He took this a step further with the idea that the body uses food to repair itself and create energy, and the amount of food someone needed depended on how much work his or her body did each day. For example, a wealthy city citizen with many servants would not need as many calories as a poor laborer working in the fields all day.

Hippocrates also believed four humors, or elements, determined the makeup of the body: blood, phlegm, black bile, and yellow bile. These four humors were each affiliated with different elements of the physical world. Blood was aligned with air, phlegm was aligned with water, black bile was aligned with Earth, and yellow bile was aligned with fire. Each person's character was determined by a unique mixture of the four humors. Someone who was cheerful was said to be sanguine, the temperament associated with a predominance of blood. Someone who was often sad, or melancholic, had a predominantly Earth-based constitution.

The Greeks did not limit their study of food to the effect it had on the body. They were also concerned with food security and food safety. To produce a consistent

Greeks were the first known people to leave a field unplanted—a form of crop rotation.

harvest that would not result in famine, the Greeks allowed some fields to go unplanted. This restored the health of the soil so it could produce a good harvest the following year.

Hippocrates saw diet, exercise, and sleep as essential to preserving a person's humoral balance, and thus his or her health. Foods in this sense were regarded as an essential part of medical treatment. In addition to the humors, Hippocrates also documented poisonous plants and his fellow Greeks' eating habits as a reference for future scholars. The Greeks consistently battled lead poisoning. Lead is a heavy metal capable of causing severe illness or death. However, the Greeks did not know lead was poisonous. They used it to line their cooking pots and wine preparation containers. The lead lining gave wine a sweet taste the Greeks used to cover up the taste of sour wine. The sweet taste was caused by a lead byproduct called lead sugar. Just one teaspoon (5 mL) of lead sugar would have been enough to give a Greek lead poisoning.

Food Science in the Roman Empire

Romans also spent a great deal of time exploring agricultural techniques and food preparation. Borrowing from the Greeks, ancient Roman doctors, such as Aulus Cornelius Celsus, classified foods as strong or weak. In the first century CE, Celsus believed wheat bread was the strongest food, followed by meat, fish, vegetables, and fruits.

However, it was the anatomist and physiologist Galen of Pergamum who dominated Roman food thought. In the early 160s, Galen used Hippocrates's theory of the four humors to develop a system of eating. Physicians in Europe and the Middle East would use Galen's nutrition theory until the 1700s. Galen asserted certain foods carried the characteristics of the four humors. Avoiding some foods while indulging in others would tip the balance of the humors in an individual, changing his or her state of health. For example, Galen said fruits, which were air (cold) and water (moist), caused fever and diarrhea. However, fruits could be used to cure someone who had too much fire (hot) and Earth (dry).

Like the Greeks, the Romans were often poisoned by the lead they used to line their cooking pots. Roman authors Ovid and Horace documented poisonous plants and Roman eating habits. At its peak, the Roman Empire sprawled across the northern coast of Africa, much of Europe, and most of the Arabian Peninsula. This meant the empire could farm and gather food from a wide area. A drought or poor harvest in one region would not affect the food security of the entire

GREEK AND ROMAN FOOD TASTERS

Food poisoning was very common in ancient Greece and Rome. Often, poisoning was unintentional, but sometimes, people tried to kill others by poisoning their food. Greek and Roman royalty regularly employed tasters to test their food for poison. The taster would eat a sample of each dish before the royalty. If the tester grew ill or died, the food was considered poisonous. The tradition of using tasters continued for 2,000 years and spread among other cultures.

empire. However, drought and poor harvests did affect the local populations, especially the millions of peasants who worked the land, since food was sent from their farmlands to city centers.

Food Science in the Middle Ages

While nutritional theory stayed consistent from the 100s CE to the 1700s, communities adopted different ways to store food. From approximately 500 to 1500, an era known as the Middle Ages, it was common for people to keep livestock in town with them instead of in fields in the country. The waste from livestock was thrown into the streets and rivers. This drew vermin and other animals into the villages, threatening the health of community members. Butchers also tended to slaughter both healthy and ill animals together and process meat that had already spoiled, subjecting the people who ate the meat to disease.

Processing and eating spoiled meat were not the only questionable eating habits in the Middle Ages. People in medieval Europe enjoyed fruits and vegetables, but fruits and vegetables were not always in season. Meat was often scarce. As a result, people often relied on bread for the majority of their daily calories. This put them at risk of starvation if a season's wheat crop was unsuccessful.

One severe example of how the success of crops could affect a medieval European's health and diet was the famine of 1316. In the early 1300s, economic conditions and unpredictable weather increased the prices of crops. In 1314, summer rains drenched crops and caused them to rot in the fields, making them inedible. In 1316, severe rains came again and once more rendered crops unusable. As a result of high prices and two unsuccessful harvests in three years, Europe experienced the worst famine in history. Approximately 10 percent of the continent's total population lost their lives to starvation.[1]

Dependence on bread led to some of the first food regulation laws. In 1202, King John of England required all loaves of bread to be the same size. Some bakers claimed their loaves were heavier than they actually were, cheating people for higher prices. King John also made it a crime to add ground peas or beans to flour to make more flour for more loaves. At the time, it was common for people

SCURVY

The diets of people in ancient times through the Renaissance often led to vitamin deficiencies and related diseases. One of the most common was scurvy, a disease caused by a lack of vitamin C. The disease was known to Greek and Roman thinkers and became common in European sailors from the Middle Ages to the 1800s. Scurvy causes gum disease, anemia, weakness, and skin hemorrhages. Scurvy is preventable and treatable by eating foods rich in vitamin C, including citrus fruits. Explorers in the 1500s noticed the symptoms of scurvy disappeared when citrus fruits were available to sailors, but this connection was not established scientifically until the 1800s.

in London to drag offending bakers through the streets and throw stones and the organs of slaughtered livestock at them.

Food Science in the Renaissance

Until the 1700s, doctors continued using Galen's nutritional theories based on the humors, but there were a few exceptions. One was the Swiss doctor Paracelsus, who wrote and studied in the 1500s. Instead of the four elements claimed in Galen's writings, Paracelsus believed all living things were made of three elements: salt, mercury, and sulphur. Paracelsus also disagreed with Galen's writings asserting that people become ill from an imbalance of humors. Instead, Paracelsus believed disease was caused by one or more of the body's organs. Galen's theories, however, continued to dominate western medicine.

Food safety remained a concern in the Renaissance. Wet weather in the spring caused fungus and mold to grow on crops left in fields during the winter. Often, humans ate these crops and then became ill. Two common diseases were ergotism and alimentary toxic aleukia. The ergot fungus grows on rye. Ergotism causes itchy, burning skin and poor circulation, often resulting in lost fingers and toes. It also causes hallucinations and seizures and can be fatal. Alimentary toxic aleukia is a disease caused by a fungus that grows on rye, millet, rice, wheat, barley, and corn. When grains with the fungus are eaten, people may suffer from fever, bleeding from the skin, nose, throat, and gums, and a suppressed immune system.

Medieval Europe's dependence on bread left many at risk for vitamin deficiencies, resulting in diseases, such as rickets.

Fungus and mold were not the only organisms making humans sick from food during the Renaissance. In 1988, researchers published a study of the preserved contents of the latrines at French King Louis XIV's country estate, where he spent time away from court between 1680 and 1715. The researchers found roundworm and tapeworm parasites present in the waste from the people who lived and worked on the estate. These parasites can cause infections and intestinal blockage. The researchers also found liver flukes in the preserved waste. Liver flukes, which are also parasites, can cause liver damage and jaundice.

Though not identified as such, food science was a much-studied field from ancient times all the way through the Renaissance in Europe. Scientists studying during the Enlightenment in the 1700s and the Industrial Revolution in the 1800s and 1900s would continue this study, building on some theories and discounting others.

Tapeworms and other parasites likely made humans sick during the Renaissance.

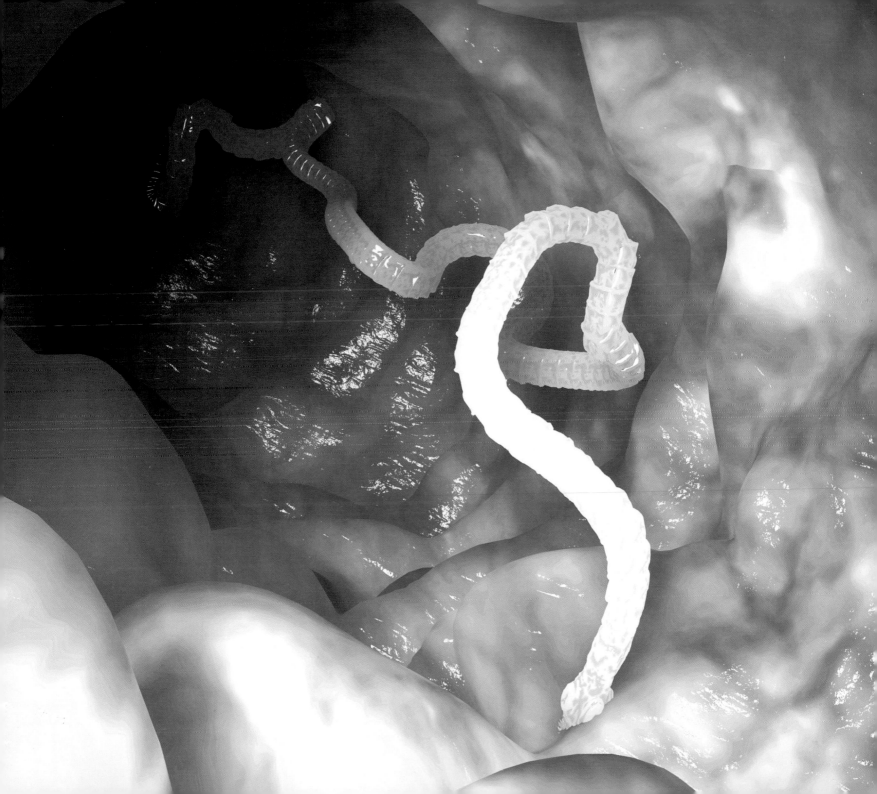

Birth of Modern
FOOD SCIENCE

$$\frac{a+b}{a} = \frac{a}{b} = 1,618$$

In the 1700s, the Industrial Revolution began in Europe. Machines replaced manual labor on farms and people moved to the city. The technological advances of the Industrial Revolution had a profound effect on how people studied, ate, and stored food.

From the 1500s through the 1700s, scientists began challenging Galen's theories of humors and nutrition. New theories were based more on observation of the human body than philosophy. One example is Andreas Vesalius, a Belgian physician and anatomist of the 1500s. Though originally a follower of Galen, Vesalius began challenging Galen's theory after conducting his own work on human anatomy. In 1543, Vesalius published *On the Fabric of the Human Body*, an illustrated textbook on anatomy. In it, he wrote the stomach was similar to a workshop that mixes food

Anatomist Andreas Vesalius challenged Galen's theories, further explaining how the body digests food.

THOMAS MALTHUS

Thomas Malthus was a historian and economist studying in the late 1700s. Observing the growing urban populations and lack of nutritious food, Malthus hypothesized population growth would outpace society's ability to produce food. He believed the world's population would grow until it was limited by lagging food production, at which point famine, war, and poor health would decrease the rate of population growth. Malthus published his ideas in "Essay on the Principle of Population as it Affects the Future Improvement of Society" in 1798. His essay was widely read and influenced economic theory, especially in Great Britain. His ideas even inspired Charles Darwin's theory of evolution.

together and moves it to the intestine. There, Vesalius argued, juices from the food passed through the veins to the liver to make blood, which was then pumped through the body.

In the 1700s, many scientists studied and developed nutritious foods for the masses, including the poor and the military. Experts considered both groups at risk for malnutrition. When the Industrial Revolution brought heavy machinery to the farming process, many farm laborers found themselves without work. They moved to cities in hopes of finding jobs. These urban newcomers discovered securing nutritious food in the city was more difficult than it was in the country. Scientists worked on products that would be affordable and nutritious. US-born British citizen Benjamin Count von Rumford, for example, claimed humans were primarily made of water. Because of this, he argued, soup was the most nutritious food. He developed a soup he believed was both nutritious and cheap to produce. The soup was made of pearl barley, potatoes, vinegar, peas, and wheat bread. Sometimes, meat was added. The soup was

Soup kitchens around the United States help bring food to millions each year.

used to feed poor workers. Some historians believe his theory of serving soup and aiding the poor may have led to the first soup kitchen.

Weather continued to have a large impact on food availability for populations around the world. In 1770, India experienced a devastating famine, which killed

FEEDING INDUSTRIAL REVOLUTION INFANTS

One of the major developments for feeding the poor was the invention of baby formula. Many poor mothers had to work all day to support their families and were unavailable to breastfeed their babies. At first, mothers relied on watered-down cow's milk to feed their infants. However, cow's milk was often contaminated. In an effort to make it safer, mothers boiled the milk to sterilize it, destroying essential nutrients. Exhausted parents often turned to products containing opium and other narcotics to keep children quiet or asleep. These products had appealing names, such as Mother's Helper, Soothing Syrup, or Atkinson & Barker's Royal Infants Preservative. Thousands of babies were given these drugs, and their sale was not banned until the 1900s.

10 million people.[1] In 1768 and 1769, the monsoons had failed to arrive on time, causing the rice crop to become dry and fail. Then, drought hit in 1770. The famine resulting from the failed rice crops affected people in the Indian regions of Bengal, Bihar, and Orissa. By September 1770, some rain fell, but it was too late to save the crop. So many people died that bodies lay unburied and unburned in the streets. Though the weather improved in 1771, not enough people survived the famine in 1770 to till the land. In the 1800s, historian W. W. Hunter studied the Bengal Famine. He noted the dire conditions people suffered: "[Peasants] sold their cattle; they sold their implements of agriculture, they devoured their seed grain, they sold their sons and daughters. . . . They ate the leaves of trees and the grass of the field and in June 1770 . . . the living were feeding on the dead."[2]

The Invention of Canning

One of the most important breakthroughs in feeding the masses came from French confectioner Nicolas Appert in the 1790s. Appert invented a way to conserve foods using heat and glass jars. First, he heated food in glass jars in a closed, sealed container similar to a pressure cooker. Once the food

By May 1770, drought and famine had killed one-third of India's population.

was almost boiling, Appert heated the food with steam and sealed the jars with hot wax and cork, preserving the food inside for years. His invention caught the attention of French research institute Society for the Encouragement of National Industry. The organization established a special committee to test Appert's techniques. They found no flaw with his method, except that the glass jars could break during the process.

With Appert's new canning technique, it was now possible for sailors, explorers, and military personnel to travel long distances with a stable, nutritious supply of food. Appert's technique was further improved by the work of British scientists Bryan Donkin and John Hall. They created the first tinned canned food in 1812. Replacing Appert's glass jars with tin cans ensured food would not be wasted by broken jars.

Though canned and tinned food was a major innovation in the 1700s and early 1800s, canned food still contained some hazards. The quality of the canned meat varied. Sometimes, the quality was so poor it made people sick. This changed once canning was moved from the laboratory or home and into factories.

Food Adulteration

During the Industrial Revolution, it became common for food producers to add substances, many of which were harmful to human health, to food products. This practice is called food adulteration. Adulteration added more substance to food, healthy or not, so sellers could market their goods at a higher profit. In England, bread bakers routinely added chalk; plaster of Paris, a mixture of lime and cement; sawdust;

Appert, Donkin, and Hall's canning innovations are still used to store and distribute food today.

bonemeal, or ground animal bones mixed with slaughterhouse waste products; or even toxic alum, used to dye fabrics and tan leather. German butchers added flour to sausage, dyeing it red so consumers would not suspect the adulteration. In Spain, olive oil often contained machine oil, and cod liver oil given to US children often contained train oil. It was also common for candymakers to add toxic chemicals to candy to create bright colors to draw in children.

Many historians believe the most outrageous instance of food adulteration was the adulteration of milk. Infants and young children consumed more milk than teens and adults during the Industrial Revolution. It was also a period of high infant mortality. Many times, sick or malnourished cows were used to produce milk, which in turn led to a sickly product often riddled with blood, pus, or mucus from an ill cow. An 1877 study of London milk found a quarter of all milk sold in the city was adulterated. In the United States, milk adulteration was, according to biophysicist Walter Gratzer, "almost universal."[3] Skimmed milk often contained poisonous lead chromate to add back the creamy color lost when the fat was skimmed out of the milk. Other common milk additives were flour, plaster of Paris, chalk, and ground rice.

Microscopist Arthur Hill Hassal analyzed food additives in the 1850s. Hassal began looking at food samples under a microscope. He discovered nearly all coffee on the market at the time had additives. Out of 34 coffee samples, Hassal found only two were pure coffee. Others contained beans, roasted corn, potato flour, or chicory—a flowering plant with roots that could be substituted for coffee beans.

Hassal began a campaign against food adulteration. He purchased foods from his local grocers and analyzed them under his microscope. He then published his findings and the addresses of the grocers—though not their names— in his reports. Hassal's work contributed to the English Parliament's passing of the Food Adulteration Act in 1860. The act established penalties for people who knowingly sold food with harmful additives. Innovations in food science during the Industrial Revolution would become the foundation of modern food science. Throughout the 1900s, scientists would build on the discoveries of the 1800s to help expand understanding of nutrition and food safety and secure the food supply for growing nations.

FOOD ADULTERATION CRITIC

Food adulteration did not escape the criticism of scientists. In the 1790s, German scientist Frederick Accum had a lab in London. Disgusted with the number of additives in foods, Accum used his laboratory to test foods he bought as a consumer for additives. Thirty years later, Accum published his findings. Accum's treatise named all the additives he found in foods. He also listed the names and addresses of the companies that supplied the chemicals. Accum's treatise was not well-received. He was run out of town and was forced to return to Germany.

Food Preservation
AND SAFETY

In the 1800s, scientists continued developing foods they believed could feed the growing number of urban poor as well as ways to make food safer and last longer. Some scientists began looking at the connection between digestion and chemistry. They came up with new theories about how the body breaks down fat and protein and what elements were present in foods. Despite these advances, people around the world continued suffering from malnutrition and famine.

More Urban Poor, More Hunger

Throughout the 1800s, England experienced a great expansion of the divide in living standards between the wealthy and the poor. While the wealthy overindulged in rich foods, the poor lacked access to fresh, nutritious food.

Famines of the 1800s in England left millions without food, forcing people to eat plants, such as seaweed.

$$\frac{a+b}{a} = \frac{a}{b} = 1.618$$

In 1834, Parliament passed the Poor Law Amendment Act. It required workhouses to provide nutritious food to inmates. They now had to serve meat, potatoes, bread, vegetable soup, cheese, and milk. A year later, another law was passed to improve the food served at prisons. Before the law went into effect, prisoners survived on bread and gruel—a soupy mixture of oatmeal boiled in milk and water—and suffered from dysentery, scurvy, and tuberculosis. The 1835 law required prisons to serve more potatoes, which are rich in vitamin C, to combat scurvy.

Liebig Applies Chemistry to Food Science

In the 1800s, scientists disagreed whether digestion was a mechanical process or a chemical one. Hundreds of years earlier, scientists such as Vesalius described digestion as a workshop, where food was moved and broken down by the organs. Now, chemists explored whether the basic chemicals in foods and the body contributed to digestion. Two of the most influential were the German chemists Johannes Peter Müller and Justus von Liebig. Müller rejected the old ideas that

In addition to his work on human nutrition, Liebig also researched the chemistry behind plant and soil life.

digestion was a mechanical process and instead argued living things digested food primarily through chemistry. However, he was not able to illustrate if or how these chemical changes occur.

Liebig was a colleague of Müller. Initially, Liebig was interested in the chemistry of animal digestion and agriculture. He was the first to explain how nutrients are chemically broken down, absorbed, and used by the body. Later, Liebig turned his attention to human nutrition.

Liebig developed two products that were popular with the public. The first was a meat extract he contended was super-nutritious. It was made from the meat of animals used to make leather. The meat was crushed between rollers. The pulp was then steam-heated for an hour. Then Liebig took out the fat, and the remaining liquid was boiled down and concentrated. That concentration was filtered once more, then sealed in sterile tins. Other scientists doubted the extract was actually nutritious. They pointed out the extract did not contain any protein or fat, which were both essential nutrients. Liebig also developed an infant formula, which hit the market in 1867. Called Liebig's Perfect Infant Food, the formula was a mixture of cow's milk, wheat flour, and malt flour. This mixture was heated with potassium bicarbonate to add potassium, an essential nutrient. But Liebig's formula did not have enough vitamins to foster healthy child development.

Understanding Proteins and Fats

Müller and Liebig were among the first scientists to study food chemistry. Other chemists soon took up the study. Dutch chemist Gerrit Jan Mulder devoted his research to proteins. He discovered protein molecules were enormous, often made up

Liebig's popular meat extract was advertised among the wealthy in the form of trade cards depicting famous events.

1 La vie de Mozart.

Premiers essais au piano à l'âge de 3 ans, 175

of hundreds of atoms. Mulder also discovered phosphorous and sulfur, in addition to carbon, nitrogen, hydrogen, and oxygen, were present in protein molecules.

French chemist Michel Eugène Chevreul studied fats. He discovered fats were actually made up of long strands of acids called fatty acids. Fatty acids contain chains of carbon and hydrogen atoms and are essential for life. Chevreul was also the first person to identify cholesterol, a waxy substance the body needs for digestion and to produce hormones and vitamin D. These discoveries of food's basic substances set the foundation for future food science breakthroughs.

Pasteur and Lister Change the World

Perhaps two of the most important discoveries of the 1800s were French scientist Louis Pasteur's discovery of microorganisms and British scientist Joseph Lister's discovery of antiseptics, or substances that kill microorganisms. These discoveries helped improve food preservation and safety. In 1860, Pasteur discovered microorganisms living in food caused food to spoil. He hypothesized that if these microorganisms were killed, the food would become safe to eat. After experimentation, he found that heating foods to 140 degrees Fahrenheit (60°C) killed most harmful microorganisms.

Lister was a surgeon in the male accident ward of the Glasgow Royal Infirmary. Before Lister's use of antiseptics in 1865, 45 percent of all surgical patients died during or as a result of their operations.[1] Lister experimented with different ways to prevent

Louis PASTEUR

Considered one of the founders of the field of microbiology, Louis Pasteur was a French chemist and microbiologist. Pasteur attended the École Normale Supérieure, where he earned his doctorate degree in 1847. In 1854, Pasteur became the dean of the science faculty at the University of Lille. There, he studied the fermentation of alcohol and how milk went sour. Just three years later, Pasteur left the University of Lille to take a position as manager and director of scientific studies at the École Normale Supérieure.

It was at the École Normale Supérieure Pasteur discovered certain microorganisms were responsible for the fermentation of different foods. Pasteur applied this germ theory to food spoilage. He discovered he could kill the microorganisms responsible for food spoilage by heating the foods to 120 to 140 degrees Fahrenheit (49 to 60°C). His method, called pasteurization, is still used today.

REFRIGERATION

Shortly before Pasteur and Lister made their discoveries, another scientist developed a way to keep food fresher longer. In 1855, Australian scientist James Harrison created a device that kept food cool. When foods cool down, it makes it more difficult for food to spoil. When liquids evaporate, they take heat with them. Harrison used this principle to create a machine that could cool ice in a process called refrigeration. Harrison tested his device on ships transporting meat from Australia to England. Though not entirely successful—the ice melted before reaching England and the food spoiled—Harrison's idea would be improved upon and used on railway cars shipping food across the United States.

infection after surgery. People believed bad air caused infection. Lister argued something else was the culprit. At first, he thought small, pollenlike particles were to blame, but then he read Pasteur's work on microorganisms and realized germs were the cause. Lister experimented with protecting the surgical site from exposure to germs. He required surgeons to clean their hands and instruments with carbolic acid, which he found to be an effective antiseptic. Soon Lister's discovery was used outside the surgical ward. Upper-class households started using his technique in kitchens to help prevent the spread of food-borne illnesses.

Food Scarcity in the 1800s

Despite improvements in food safety and the world's understanding of nutrition, millions of people continued to die from malnutrition and starvation throughout the 1800s. Germany faced a food crisis in the latter part of the century due to poor harvests. One-third of Ethiopia's population died between 1888 and 1892 due to famine. A famine in China between 1876 and 1879 killed between 9 and 13 million people. Famines in India in 1866, 1869, and between 1876 and 1878 killed approximately 7.5 million people.[2]

Though it did not result in the most loss of life, one of the most studied famines from the 1800s was the Irish Potato Famine. In 1845, a fungus destroyed the potato crop in Ireland. The poor harvest caused a famine in the country for the next ten years. Between 1845 and 1855, more than 1 million Irish people died and 2 million immigrated to other countries to escape the famine.[3] People who were unable to move often succumbed to a condition called famine fever, a collective term for the diseases of malnutrition and starvation. These included dysentery, cholera, scurvy, typhus, and lice infestations.

The 1800s were a period of discovery and innovation in food science. Scientists began considering how chemistry played a role in digestion and nutrition and discovered the building blocks of proteins and fats. Pasteur and Lister made great strides in food safety. Yet people across the world continued to die from malnutrition. Further innovations in nutrition, food safety, and food security awaited the world as it entered the 1900s.

MAGNIFICENT MARGARINE

During the 1860s, the French navy was in need of an alternative to butter, which spoiled on long trips at sea. In 1869, French chemist Hippolyte Mège-Mouriès invented the first synthetic food, oleomargarine. Mège-Mouriès's invention was the precursor to modern margarine and was made from dissolving beef fat in the enzymes from a sheep's stomach. From this substance, Mège-Mouriès skimmed the fat, which he then treated with milk, sodium bicarbonate, and chopped up cow's udder for a buttery taste. His invention was close in taste to butter but lacked a creamy color.

The Government GETS INVOLVED

$$\frac{a+b}{a} = \frac{a}{b} = 1.618$$

The years between 1900 and the beginning of World War I (1914–1918) were productive in the study of food science. Researchers began uncovering the role vitamins and minerals play in the human diet. Meanwhile, citizen advocates began pushing for stricter food production and food safety regulations. During this time, US federal lawmakers passed the first food safety and food marketing laws.

Vitamins and Minerals

In the 1890s, Christiaan Eijkman, a Dutch military physician stationed in the colony of Java, was asked to look into the cause of beriberi. Beriberi is a disease that causes difficulty in walking, loss of muscle function, numbness in the hands and feet, and chronic pain. Today, scientists know beriberi is caused by a lack of vitamin B.

Upton Sinclair's 1906 *The Jungle* was influential in passing the first US federal food safety laws.

THE JUNGLE

BY
UPTON SINCLAIR

Beriberi Birds

The birds used in Eijkman's beriberi research developed symptoms of the disease similar to those humans displayed. The birds fell over and were unable to get back on their feet. Those that did not fall over stood with their legs spread apart. In the later stages of the disease, the birds were unable to eat.

But at the time, scientists believed a microorganism caused beriberi. Eijkman was tasked with identifying which one. His research helped uncover quite a different cause.

To conduct his studies, Eijkman injected chickens with blood from someone believed to be infected with beriberi. He found beriberi did develop in injected birds—but only if the birds were fed white rice. White rice is rice with its outer skin removed. It is popular in tropical places such as Java because rice keeps longer without its bran exterior. When Eijkman added the bran skin to the birds' diet, their symptoms of beriberi disappeared. Eijkman's hypothesis was that the high starch level of white rice was poisonous if the branny part was removed. To double-check his work, Eijkman looked at the health records of the prisons on Java. He found that in prisons where white rice was served, one prisoner in 39 had beriberi. In prisons where rice was served with bran intact, that number tumbled to one in 10,000.[1]

Though Eijkman had discovered the bran exterior of rice was an important factor in preventing beriberi, his hypothesis as to why was incorrect. Another scientist, Gerrit Grijns, took up Eijkman's work in 1896 after Eijkman returned to Holland. Grijns wanted to test Eijkman's theory about the toxicity of high starch levels in rice. To do so, he conducted an experiment on chickens. He wanted to see if the chickens would

Christiaan EIJKMAN

As a young man, Christiaan Eijkman attended the Military Medical School of the University of Amsterdam. He took several posts as a medical officer in the Dutch colonies of Java and Sumatra. While serving a post, Eijkman contracted malaria. During his recovery, Eijkman met two doctors who asked him to help them with their investigation of beriberi in the tropics.

Though these doctors soon had to return to the Netherlands, Eijkman accepted the position of director at a laboratory on Java. Here, he conducted research on the physiology of the native people. Europeans believed there was a difference in the metabolism, perspiration, and respiratory systems of tropical populations and themselves. Eijkman's research proved there was no such difference. However, his greatest work was on the cause of beriberi, for which he won the Nobel Prize in 1929.

develop beriberi if they were fed foods that were not starchy. Grijns fed his chickens only meat that had been subjected to high heat and pressure to sterilize it. Despite the lack of starch in the meat, his birds developed beriberi. When Grijns added beans and the bran exteriors of rice into the chickens' diet, they recovered.

Grijns concluded foods must contain "substances which cannot be absent without serious injury to the peripheral nervous system."[2] Grijns had discovered and described the concept of vitamins. Other scientists would continue studying and discovering the various vitamins necessary to human health throughout the next few decades.

Protesting Dirty Slaughterhouses

Around the time Eijkman and Grijns studied beriberi and vitamins in Java and Europe, a group of dedicated women were protesting the disgusting conditions of New York City's slaughterhouses. The Ladies' Health Protective Association conducted inspections of Manhattan's slaughterhouses and found dried blood on the floors

CONGRESS INVESTIGATES SLAUGHTERHOUSES

Sinclair's *The Jungle* reported on the conditions of slaughterhouses and caused public outcry, as illustrated in an excerpt from a 1906 congressional report:

"An absence of cleanliness was . . . found everywhere in the handling of meat being prepared for the various meat-food products. . . . In some of the largest establishments, sides [of meat] that are sent to . . . the boning room are thrown in a heap on the floor. The workers climb over these heaps of meat, select the pieces they wish, and . . . throw them down upon the dirty floor beside their working bench. . . . Moreover, men were seen to climb from the floor and stand, with shoes dirty from the refuse from the floors, on the tables upon which the meat was handled."[3]

and piles of rotting meat onto which fresh meat was thrown on its way to market. The women took their findings to the slaughterhouse owners and, if no actions were taken to clean up the slaughterhouses, to the city's Board of Health.

Halfway across the country, the stockyards and slaughterhouses in Chicago, Illinois, came under similar scrutiny. Journalist Upton Sinclair studied the unsanitary working conditions of the stockyards. Sinclair's 1906 novel *The Jungle* revealed his observations.

First US Food Safety Laws

The publication of *The Jungle* created public outcry, and the federal government took action. In 1906, Congress passed two laws: the Federal Meat Inspection Act and the Pure Food and Drug Act. The Meat Inspection Act set standards for butchering and required a meat inspector to be present at a slaughterhouse whenever it was in operation. This led to daily slaughterhouse inspections, which forced slaughterhouses to clean up their practices, increasing food safety and reducing foodborne illness.

THE USDA

The Pure Food and Drug Act and the Federal Meat Inspection Act of 1906 were the first federal laws specifically targeting food safety. But 44 years prior, President Abraham Lincoln had established the first government department devoted to the study of agriculture and food. In 1862, Lincoln signed a bill into law establishing the United States Department of Agriculture (USDA). At the time, approximately 50 percent of Americans lived on farms.[4] The department helped these farmers by providing seed and other support. After the Federal Meat Inspection Act passed, the USDA became responsible for inspecting the nation's meat products.

The Pure Food and Drug Act was enacted on June 30, 1906. Prior to its passage, several states had established their own food safety laws. It was common at the time for people to become sick and even die because their food was contaminated. Processed foods and canned goods were known to contain bacteria, including salmonella and *E. coli*. The Pure Food and Drug Act made it illegal to sell, produce, or transport adulterated food, liquor, and drugs. It also made it illegal to misbrand foods. Seven years later, Congress passed the Gould Amendment. It required companies to label food packaging with the weight, numerical count, or an alternative measure of food products.

In the early 1900s, scientists made strides in the study of vitamins and nutrition, while citizens pushed for food safety regulations and reform. These innovations would help guide future food science research and food production.

The Meat Inspection Act ensured sanitary standards were being met in slaughterhouses.

US V. LEXINGTON MILL & ELEVATOR COMPANY

In 1914, the US Supreme Court issued its first ruling on food additives in the *US v. Lexington Mill & Elevator Company* court case. The ruling concerned bleached flour that had been treated with nitrogen peroxide gas. The Lexington Mill used the gas to purify and bleach the flour. The government argued the use of the gas constituted food adulteration, which was illegal under the Pure Food and Drug Act. However, the court ruled that for an additive to be illegal, the government must prove it was hazardous to human health. It noted it was not enough for an additive to be present for the food to be deemed illegal. This ruling affected food law until 1938 and the passage of the Federal Food, Drug, and Cosmetic Act. The new law required companies to prove an additive was safe before a food hit the market.

Great War, Great Depression, GREAT SCIENCE

$$\frac{a+b}{a} = \frac{a}{b} = 1.618$$

On June 28, 1914, a Serbian assassin killed Austria-Hungarian archduke Franz Ferdinand in Sarajevo, Bosnia. The assassination was the catalyst for the worst war humanity had experienced at the time, World War I, which was also called the Great War. World War I involved the major imperial powers of the time—the United Kingdom, Russia, Austria-Hungary, France, Germany, and Turkey—and their allies. Approximately 8.5 million soldiers died from wounds or diseases acquired while fighting.[1] For the major players involved, the war not only required a capable military

Food lines were common during the early 1900s as food shortages gripped the nation.

FEEDING THE DOUGHBOYS

The United States entered World War I in 1917, just one year before the conflict ended. Like Britain and Germany, the US government had to plan how it would feed its soldiers, who were nicknamed doughboys. According to the plan, each soldier was to receive bread, beer, milk, and one pound (0.5 kg) of protein every day. Additionally, doughboys enjoyed butter, candy, and potatoes. Food was brought to soldiers in the field on carts, and makeshift bakeries were set up to supply troops with bread. One historian called the American forces, "the best-fed army in World War I."[3]

and new military technology. It also required innovative ways to keep soldiers and civilians at home fed.

On October 29, 1929, 11 years after World War I ended, the United States experienced the worst economic panic it had ever seen. The New York Stock Exchange crashed, culminating in a loss of $25 billion, which would equal $319 billion today.[2] Companies laid off workers and cut wages, leading to mass unemployment. Economic circumstances made it difficult for people to put food on the table. The government began programs to help people afford food and continued passing laws to improve food safety. The Great War and the Great Depression helped shape the study of food science between 1914 and 1939.

Rationing and the Great War

Countries on both sides during World War I had to develop a plan to feed their military and their civilian populations. British soldiers were allowed 10 ounces (283 g) of meat per day, as well as 8 ounces (227 g) of vegetables. Their German counterparts received 13 ounces (369 g) of meat and 4.5 to 9 ounces (128 to 255 g) of vegetables. However, as the war progressed, food became harder to come by. Though troops on both sides saw decreases in rations throughout the war, civilians were subjected to severe rationing from the start. Blockades prevented supplies from reaching the citizens of the countries in combat. In Russia and Turkey, the people and resources to maintain the countries' food distribution processes were given over to the war effort, leaving civilians to fend for themselves. Starvation was the result.

Germany tried to control the production, sale, and consumption of foods, but its efforts led to malnutrition and starvation for many Germans. Many of the foods the government substituted for unavailable foods were not nutritious. At the end of 1914, the German government encouraged citizens to adopt a potato diet. The potatoes soon ran out, so the government ordered the slaughter of all the pigs in the country so the potatoes used to feed the pigs and the pigs themselves could be used to feed people instead.

The winter of 1915 to 1916 was particularly tough for German citizens. Nicknamed the "turnip winter," many Germans resorted to using turnips to make bread, cakes, coffee, jam, and even beer.[5] In 1916, a flour shortage led British army cooks to use ground turnips, which caused diarrhea.

Meatless Mondays

During World War I, the United States asked its citizens not fighting overseas to conserve food and get creative in the kitchen to support the war effort. It marketed the ideas of "Meatless Mondays" and "Wheatless Wednesdays," encouraging people to forgo meat and bread one day a week. The government produced pamphlets with recipes to help cooks create meals that did not include meat or wheat.

Goldberger's Pursuit of Pellagra's Cause

In the early 1900s, poor rural people in the southern United States were experiencing symptoms of the disease pellagra. In 1912, there were 30,000 cases in South Carolina alone.[4] The condition causes skin irritation and diarrhea. In extreme cases, it causes dementia, delusions, and death. The causes of pellagra stumped scientists for years. Most scientists believed the condition was caused by an infection and could be spread from person to person. In 1914, Surgeon General Rupert Blue asked surgeon Dr. Joseph Goldberger to study pellagra and find its true cause.

Goldberger conducted a study on prison inmates in Mississippi. Twelve volunteers were housed in a sanitized building and given clean clothes to wear to eliminate the possibility of infection. Then, they were given meals that mimicked what the rural poor ate: cornbread, grits, molasses, and kale leaves. In a few weeks, the volunteers began experiencing fatigue, confusion, and mouth sores. Five months into the study, half the volunteers showed symptoms of pellagra. Goldberger theorized pellagra was caused by deficiencies in the diet, including lack of protein and minerals. When Goldberger published his results, he was considered a food science hero. Yet some southern doctors were still not convinced. They believed the condition was caused by infection. To convince them, Goldberger and seven volunteers spent time in a pellagra hospital, exposing themselves to the bodily fluids of pellagra patients. None of the volunteers were infected by the disease. Goldberger's theory was confirmed in 1937.

Goldberger was nominated five times for a Nobel Prize for his work on pellagra.

MINISTRY OF FOOD.

BREACHES OF THE RATIONING ORDER

The undermentioned convictions have been recently obtained:—

Court	Date	Nature of Offence	Result
HENDON - -	29th Aug., 1918	Unlawfully obtaining and using ration books -	3 Months' Imprisonment
WEST HAM -	29th Aug., 1918	Being a retailer & failing to detach proper number of coupons	Fined £20
SMETHWICK -	22nd July, 1918	Obtaining meat in excess quantities - - -	Fined £50 & £5 5s. costs
OLD STREET -	4th Sept., 1918	Being a retailer selling to unregistered customer	Fined £72 & £5 5s. costs
OLD STREET -	4th Sept., 1918	Not detaching sufficient coupons for meat sold -	Fined £25 & £2 2s. costs
CHESTER-LE-STREET	4th Sept., 1918	Being a retailer returning number of registered customers in excess of counterfoils deposited - - - -	Fined £50 & £3 3s. costs
HIGH WYCOMBE	7th Sept., 1918	Making false statement on application for and using Ration Books unlawfully - - - - - - -	Fined £40 & £6 4s. costs

During World War I, British civilians were penalized for using more ration coupons than were allowed.

That same year, a common meal for a British soldier was pea soup with chunks of horse meat. The Germans instituted a policy of one meatless meal per week starting in June 1916.

The United Kingdom had more success in controlling its civilian food supply. The country suffered from lack of imported food due to German submarine attacks.

Britain was also lacking the labor and fertilizer to tend all its fields since the men and nitrates used to make fertilizer went to the war effort. The government, however, employed every able-bodied civilian to fuel its war and agricultural efforts. They put people to work in farm fields and required home gardens. The government then adopted a ration system for civilians in 1918. The rations were the same for people whether they were rich or poor. For the first time in more than a century, the divide between rich and poor began decreasing.

Discoveries of the 1920s

After World War I, scientists were able to once again focus on nutrition. They built upon the vitamin and mineral research of Eijkman, Grijns, and others to uncover the nutritional causes of common conditions such as rickets, pellagra, and goiters. For example, by the 1930s, the discovery that vitamin D could prevent rickets had nearly eradicated the disease.

In the 1920s, milk pasteurization became standardized across the nation. The federal Public Health Service worked with the state of Alabama to standardize its milk sanitation program. Although the program, which was called the Grade "A" Pasteurized Milk Ordinance, was voluntary, it eventually became the standard for all milk safety laws in the country.

Crowds panic in an attempt to trade stocks on Wall Street on October 24, 1929.

The Great Depression

The US stock market crashed on October 29, 1929, marking the beginning of the Great Depression. The financial crisis of the Great Depression affected both agriculture and people's wallets. Though many farmers produced enough food, families could not afford to purchase it. In the early 1930s, the prices of wheat and other foods considered commodities dropped. At the same time, food companies were not purchasing these foods because they did not have the funds. The result was a surplus of food commodities. Meanwhile, individuals and families were struggling financially and having trouble affording food.

In response to these problems, the federal government bought up a lot of the agricultural surpluses and announced in 1933 that it would give these surpluses away to unemployed people and needy families. The program was a success, and two years later, the government was distributing surplus foods through home delivery and grocery stores.

Food Regulation in the 1930s

Depression-era lawmakers enacted legislation that affected how food was processed, marketed, and distributed. In 1930, the Food, Drug, and Insecticide Administration's name was shortened to the Food and Drug Administration (FDA). That same year, lawmakers passed the McNary-Mapes Amendment. It approved standards the FDA had proposed regarding canned food. The change allowed the FDA to

ORANGE AND BLUE

The USDA rolled out the first food stamp program in 1939, which lasted through 1943. It offered needy families two types of stamps: blue and orange. Blue stamps could be used each month to purchase surplus foods. Families purchased orange stamps at face value. In return, they received half the amount they purchased in blue stamps for free. They could use the orange stamp to purchase any type of food, not just surpluses.

THE FIRST STANDARDS

The FDA was quick to take action after the Food, Drug, and Cosmetic Act was passed. In 1939, it issued the first food standards. The standards targeted the identity, quality, and fill-of-container of canned tomatoes, tomato paste, and tomato puree. The next foods to become subject to FDA standards were jams and jellies. By the late 1950s, many foods had to meet FDA standards, including flour, cereals, milk, cheese, and eggs.

enforce standards of quality and fill-of-container for canned foods. Fill-of-container standards mandated how full a container must be and how it is measured.

In 1938, lawmakers passed the Federal Food, Drug, and Cosmetic Act to improve food and drug safety. The Food, Drug, and Cosmetic Act required food, drug, and cosmetic companies to prove the additives in their products are safe. It also required foods that imitated other foods, such as margarine, to be labeled as such. The law also made it illegal for companies to make false claims about their products. The act gave the FDA the power to hold companies accountable in the courts.

The Great War and Great Depression made an impact on food security and safety. The years between 1914 and 1939 also ushered in a new era of federal food regulation in the United States. But more innovations in food science—and tragedies in food security—were to come when Germany invaded Poland in 1939, starting the bloodshed of World War II (1939–1945).

Under regulations of the Food, Drug, and Cosmetic Act, women test facial cream in the late 1930s.

Chapter Seven

The Rise of AGRIBUSINESS

$$\frac{a+b}{a} = \frac{a}{b} = 1.618$$

In 1939, the world entered World War II, a global conflict that lasted until 1945. Millions of people were involved, including those on the front lines, those on the home front, and those interned or imprisoned. All were affected by countries' ability—or inability—to provide food. After the war, Europe struggled to rebuild its food system, while the United States experienced a period of immense growth and innovation in food science. Throughout the 1960s and 1970s, the United States and other countries made great strides in the quality and safety of their food. Innovative new products, such as freeze-dried food and milk with a long shelf life, became available. New technologies, such as irrigation systems, made it possible for farmers to produce more food and avoid the effects of drought. Food science became more and more specialized and complex.

A shopkeeper in the United Kingdom marks off ration coupons for a housewife in 1943 after she receives her allotted rations.

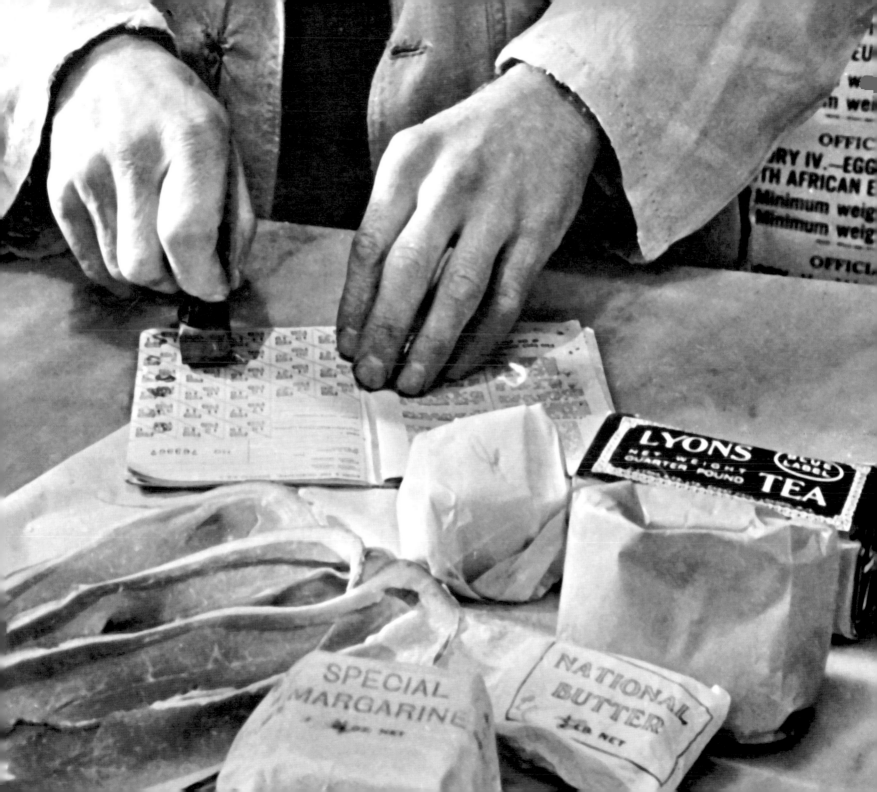

World War II: A Time of Scarcity

Food played a major role throughout World War II. Across the world, approximately 20 million people died from malnutrition, starvation, and related diseases.[1] This is approximately 500,000 more than the number of soldiers who lost their lives on the battlefield. Warring countries blockaded others, restricting access to food. Countries took advantage of the food in the countries they were invading.

In all countries, food fueled the war effort. Countries had to increase their agricultural output while farm laborers entered the military forces, factories built weapons instead of tractors, and fertilizer ingredients went to making explosives. Many civilians worked long hours in factories, which meant they had to expend more calories than usual every day. In Britain and the United States, many people kept vegetable gardens at home to supplement their daily rations. In the Soviet Union, lack of working heat and electricity meant many had to find firewood for warmth and cooking.

During the war, US citizens were asked to plant and maintain their own gardens, known as victory gardens, to help produce food.

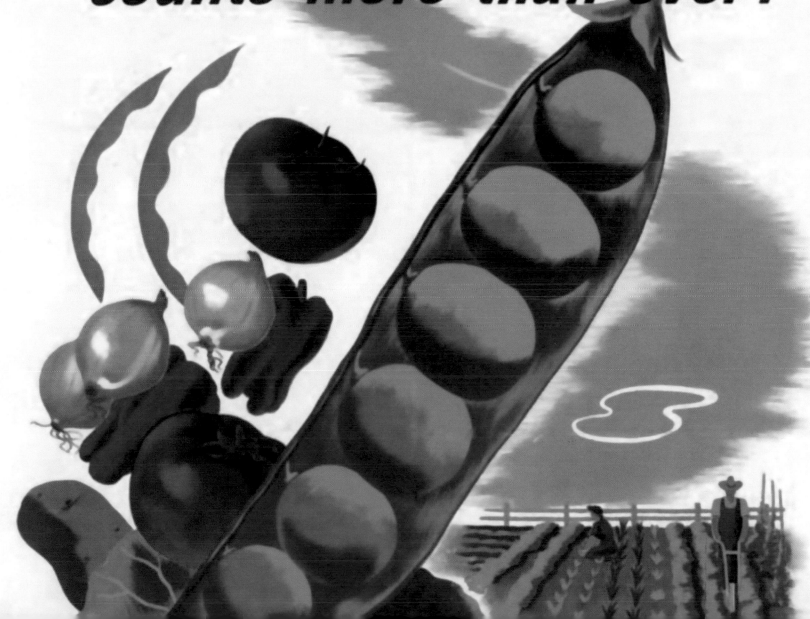

YOUR VICTORY GARDEN
counts more than ever!

The two sides of the war, the Allied and Axis powers, had different views of the value of food. The Allied powers of the United Kingdom and the United States believed it was the government's responsibility to provide nutritious food for their troops and secure the food supply for civilian workers. The Axis powers of Germany, the Soviet Union, and Japan, on the other hand, believed troops and civilian workers were expendable. While all countries used the science of nutrition in the war effort, these different views influenced each country's approach to food security.

Producing Food on the Mainland

The United States was in a unique position to provide food for both its military and civilian workforce. Unlike the countries of Europe and East Asia, the US mainland was not under threat of invasion. This meant farmland was safe from being destroyed or used by the enemy. Farmers could continue working the land and getting food to market. To support the war effort, food scientists researched how to improve the packaging and transport of food. They also developed new ways to fortify foods with vitamins and minerals and process foods to lengthen their shelf lives.

In Britain, the government conducted a program to convert lands used to raise livestock for meat to farmland for potatoes and wheat. The program also increased the number of acres (hectares) available to farm. This helped Britain rely less on imports from other countries, which made enemy blockades less effective against its food supply.

While food supplies were secure and supported by government in the United States and Britain, other countries had a more difficult time feeding their armies and their civilian workforce. The Japanese government, like that of the Soviet Union and Germany, believed its troops were expendable. As a result, 60 percent of the 1.74 million Japanese soldiers who died in World War II succumbed to starvation, not combat.[2] There are accounts of Japanese soldiers resorting to eating wild grasses to sustain themselves on the battlefield.

Under Adolf Hitler, the German government deliberately starved various groups of people. During its invasion of Poland, the German government confined the Jewish people living in Warsaw to one portion of the city and rationed the inhabitants to a meager 800 calories per day. As a result, people in the Warsaw Ghetto starved to death. Despite these desperate circumstances, several Jewish physicians took their situation as an opportunity to study and document the effects of starvation on the human body. The study was the first of its kind, and the physicians were of the opinion that

THE WARSAW GHETTO STUDY

Led by Dr. Israel Milejkowski, the Warsaw Ghetto starvation observation took place in three stages: the loss of body fat, the withering of skin and tissues, and general wasting away. The physicians found many starvation victims lost half their body mass before perishing. Many experienced muscle loss and bone weakness so severe bones could break at the slightest pressure. In addition to these observations, the group recorded blood pressure, blood volume, nitrogen and mineral metabolism, and water and electrolyte balance among the victims.

if they were going to die, the facts should be left behind for the world to see and understand after the war ended.

The First Recommended Dietary Allowances

During World War II, the United States developed and issued its first recommended dietary allowances (RDAs) for essential nutrients. The standards, developed by the Committee on Food and Nutrition under the National Academy of Science, prompted many other countries and international organizations to develop dietary standards of their own. Initially, the committee was tasked with advising the government on food issues concerning the war effort. After the end of the war, it continued advising the government under a different name, the Food and Nutrition Board.

The committee developed a tentative set of standards, which recommended daily allowances for nutrients such as calories, protein, vitamin A, B-vitamins, vitamin D, calcium, and iron. The committee then sent their standards to nutrition experts for review. With the experts' input, the committee published their finalized RDAs in 1943.

From War Rations to Years of Plenty

In the United States, the period after World War II was a time of plenty. The war had jump-started the country's economy, and young men were returning home ready to start families and earn and spend money. Between 1945 and 1949, Americans purchased 5.5 million stoves and 20 million refrigerators.[4] Devastated by the war, Europe faced a longer road to recovery. However, by the late 1940s rationing had ended in many countries. In the 1950s, farmers in developed nations abandoned many traditional methods in favor of using new farm machinery that allowed them to grow more on less land.

These technological advances changed farming methods in the United States. By the 1970s, traditional family farms began disappearing and large industrial farms became common. Due to the strong economy, farmers could afford better machinery. Scientists developed innovative center pivot irrigation systems that protected crops from the effects of drought. Meanwhile, other scientists were developing ways to improve crops and pesticides. One example was DDT, or dichloro-diphenyl-trichloroethane, the first synthetic insecticide. DDT was a powerful and effective insecticide. But by the 1960s, people began raising concerns about how DDT affected the environment, including wildlife. After a decade-long debate, the US Environmental Protection Agency banned the use of DDT, which took effect in 1973.

The result of the innovations in agriculture were farms that produced more crops per acre (hectare) of farmland, increasing competition between farmers. Individual farms dwindled as larger agricultural companies bought up the land. These large farms needed to work more and more land to survive in the competitive economy. This led to fewer—but larger—farms throughout the next few decades. The companies that owned these larger farms became very profitable. They gave rise to the concept of agribusiness, or farming guided by commercial and economic principles. These principles embraced the specialization of crops and incorporating new technology.

The decades of the 1940s to the 1970s brought both challenging years and years of plenty. Many innovations in food science were ushered in by World War II and during the years that followed. As the world entered the 1980s, people began abandoning their stoves for microwaves. Demand increased for products that were both nutritious and convenient.

In the years following World War II, purchases such as stoves were considered acts of US patriotism.

Chapter Eight

Emergence of
THE FOOD LABEL

$$\frac{a+b}{a} = \frac{a}{b} = 1.618$$

S ince the 1980s, food science has been influenced by consumer demand and continuing research on the health effects of different nutrients such as fat, salt, and carbohydrates. Some of this research has been fueled by the rise of obesity in the United States and in other countries where people eat an Americanized diet.

In the late 1970s, a special committee in the US Congress recommended a set of new dietary goals for Americans. The goals recommended Americans eat less refined sugar, saturated fat, salt, and cholesterol and more whole grains, fruits, and vegetables. They also recommended people substitute low-fat foods, such as nonfat dairy products, for full-fat ones.

In addition to recommending daily allowances of foods and nutrients, the goals also discussed energy balance. Energy balance is the idea that all the calories

Despite rising rates of obesity in wealthy nations, developing countries still face food scarcity.

78

1980 DIETARY GUIDELINES

The pamphlet outlining the 1980 dietary guidelines had seven general recommendations. It told US adults to eat a variety of foods, keep a healthy weight, avoid fat and cholesterol, avoid excess sugar, avoid excess salt, and drink alcohol only in moderation. It recommended foods rich in vitamins, minerals, and other essential nutrients, such as vegetables, meat, poultry, and whole grains. It also gave recommendations for ideal weight for adult men and women.

someone eats must be burned off by the body. If someone ate more calories than he or she used up, he or she would gain weight. Conversely, consuming fewer calories than needed would cause one to lose weight. These dietary goals recommended people eat only as many calories as they used to avoid gaining weight.

The dietary goals recommended in the late 1970s were initially met with controversy, both from food companies and food scientists. Both companies and scientists were skeptical about whether the science upon which the goals were based was credible. In 1980, to help address these concerns, the government issued a brochure called *Nutrition and Your Health: Dietary Guidelines for Americans*. The brochure outlined how to incorporate healthy foods such as vegetables and whole grains into one's diet. It also gave advice on how to limit or avoid fat, cholesterol, and salt.

Despite the guidelines outlined in the brochure, the *Dietary Guidelines for Americans* continued to face criticism. After several revisions in 1980, 1985, and 1990, however, the guidelines became a resource for consumers and physicians on what constituted a healthy, balanced diet. Though not all scientists agreed with them, the dietary guidelines helped shape food products in the United States throughout the next several decades.

Consumers Demand Convenience

In the 1980s in the United States and Europe, consumers demanded food products that fit their new, busy lifestyles. It was becoming more common for both men and women to work outside the home. Gone were the days when most women stayed at home and had an hour or two to prepare a meal from scratch.

Instead, people desired food that could be prepared in a matter of minutes without turning on the oven. In part due to the recommendations in the *Dietary Guidelines for Americans*, they also desired food that was tasty as well as low in fat and calories. This demand gave rise to highly processed convenience foods that could be frozen and reheated in microwaves. Companies came out with new products such as microwave popcorn, boxed pasta mixes, prewashed and cut salad greens, and frozen dinners. People

THE MARVELOUS MICROWAVE

Microwave ovens transformed the way people prepared and ate food. Microwave ovens use radio energy to heat food. Their technology guides and traps the radio energy until it is absorbed by the food. Engineer Percy LeBaron Spencer discovered microwaves could heat foods in 1946. But it was not until the 1960s that microwave ovens were available to the public. Once they hit the market, they were sold by the millions. With microwave ovens commonplace in homes, convenience foods that could be easily heated up or cooked in microwaves cropped up on store shelves. Cookbooks devoted to microwave oven cooking became popular.

discovered they could now purchase fruit juice in convenient, one-serving boxes. The trend toward convenient, processed foods continued throughout the 1980s and into the 1990s and 2000s.

The Nutritional Labeling and Education Act

In 1990, Congress passed the Nutritional Labeling and Education Act. It required the FDA to develop new nutritional labels for use on food products. Throughout the 1980s, people had become more interested in nutrition and food quality. Both consumers and companies showed interest in having the government require nutritional labeling for food products. In 1991, the FDA proposed 26 different regulations for nutrition labels to Congress. After deliberating and considering comments from food scientists and the food industry, Congress came up with final regulations. The final Nutrition Facts panel label was announced in January 1993, a year before the Nutritional Labeling and Education Act required food products to display the label.

In 2014, 20 years after the first Nutrition Facts label went into effect, the FDA proposed several changes to the panel label. One change was to update the serving size requirements so they were more in line with what people consumed in 2014. The FDA also recommended increasing the font size of the calories and serving sizes to make them more prominent. Just like the labels created in the early 1990s, the

Total Carbohydrate 12g	**4%**
Dietary Fiber 1g	**4%**
Sugars 1g	
Protein 24g	

Vitamin A 1%	•	**Vitamin C** 2%
Calcium 2%	•	**Iron** 5%

*Percent Daily Values are based on a 2,000 calorie diet. Your daily values may be higher or lower

In 2014, the FDA proposed adding more information to nutritional labels, such as a food's added sugar content as well as the amount of potassium and vitamin D in the food.

new labels went through a comments and revision period before being adopted by the FDA.

Food Science Developments in the 2000s

By the start of the 2000s, it was generally accepted that eating too many calories and too much fat and cholesterol led to obesity and heart disease. An entire diet industry had developed to help people avoid fat and count calories. Most of these diets recommended people eat low-fat or nonfat dairy foods. Food companies produced snack and dessert foods that were low-fat or nonfat. These diets and food products remained popular into the 2010s.

In the early 2000s, however, scientists began reexamining the low-fat, low-calorie conventional wisdom that had dominated nutrition science and diets for decades. They turned their attention to the effects of carbohydrates on the body. Some studies compared diets in which carbohydrates were restricted to those that restricted calories and fat. They found low-carbohydrate diets resulted in more weight loss than the low-fat, low-calorie diets.

In addition to research on low-carbohydrate diets, some food scientists looked into the effect sugar has on the body. Research has shown the body breaks down the various sugars, such as galactose, glucose, and fructose, differently. The liver breaks

LOW-CARB DIETS

In the 2010s, low-carbohydrate diets became increasingly popular. Most low-carb diets restrict consumption of grain foods. Instead, people eat protein and full-fat foods for energy, plus lots of vegetables and sometimes fruits. One of the earliest low-carb diets was developed by Dr. Robert Atkins, who wrote a book outlining the diet in 1972. In the 2000s, the South Beach low-carb diet became popular. More recently, people are adopting gluten-free or paleo diets. Gluten is a protein found in grain foods. Some people are sensitive to gluten and can become sick. Gluten-free diets became popular with these people and others trying to avoid grains. The paleo diet is based on what some practitioners believe human ancestors ate tens of thousands of years ago. Generally, followers of the paleo diet do not eat processed foods, grain foods, and dairy because they were not available to prehistoric humans. Instead, they eat lots of vegetables, fruits, and meat.

galactose down to glucose. Glucose is what cells in the body use for energy. The liver also breaks down fructose. However, instead of being used as energy by cells, fructose is stored as fat. Consuming too much sugar can lead to liver disease, obesity, diabetes, and heart disease.

The American Heart Association recommends women consume no more than six teaspoons (30 g) of sugar per day and men no more than nine (45 g). In 2012, the average American ate approximately 22 teaspoons (110 g) of sugar per day.[1] Sugar has addictive properties that make it difficult for people to reduce their sugar consumption or give up eating it altogether. The new research into sugar and its effects on the body has spurred a debate on whether sugar is a toxic substance that drives obesity, diabetes, and other diseases.

World of Plenty, World of Scarcity

In addition to tackling the rise in obesity in developed and developing countries, food scientists also attempt to find new ways to feed millions who suffer from malnutrition. Plumpy'Nut is one innovation helping feed millions of malnourished children. Scientists research ways to improve crop yields and make crops more resistant to drought or flooding as well. Some solutions include seeds that are resistant to severe weather and disease and providing farmers with the tools and knowledge to help them increase production. As scientists continue to make advancements in food science, they will find the solutions to these and other problems.

High-Fructose Corn Syrup

It would be difficult to name a product that has had more of an impact on the modern diet than high-fructose corn syrup. The Illinois Farm Bureau estimated the average American ate or drank 35.7 pounds (16 kg) of high-fructose corn syrup in 2009.[2]

In 1957, scientists Richard O. Marshall and Earl R. Kooi discovered an enzyme that could convert the glucose in cornstarch to fructose. In the lab, they isolated glucose molecules from cornstarch, creating corn syrup. They then used the enzyme to convert some of the glucose molecules to fructose molecules. Fructose, like glucose, is a simple sugar. The corn syrup they were left with had more fructose in it than usual, hence the name high-fructose corn syrup. Three years later, Marshall and Kooi patented the process for making high-fructose corn syrup.

Since 1971, high-fructose corn syrup has been used as a sweetener in hundreds of food products. Often, it replaces cane or beet sugar. High-fructose corn syrup made it cheaper to produce processed food products. But many food science researchers and public health officials believe the syrup causes health problems, such as obesity, because it contains higher levels of fructose.

Soft drinks contain high-fructose corn syrup, as do other popular foods such as cereals, tomato sauce, and frozen pizza.

The Future of
FOOD SCIENCE

$$\frac{a+b}{a} = \frac{a}{b} = 1.618$$

Though people have been studying food for thousands of years, there is still a lot to learn about how the body uses nutrients in foods, how to keep foods safe, and how to ensure everyone around the globe has access to healthy food. Future food scientists will continue work in these areas. As scientists innovate, they will apply different scientific disciplines to the study of food. Research on the human genome, genetic engineering, biotechnology, microbiology, and computer technology all have a role to play in the study of food.

The Human Genome and Obesity

In 2011, approximately one in six US children and one in three US adults were obese.[1] Obesity can lead to several serious health conditions, including diabetes, heart disease, and cancer. Most people believe obesity is chiefly caused by eating too many

With portion sizes increasing, many food scientists are looking for ways to help combat obesity.

Some food scientists believe genes may play a role in how the body processes and stores energy from food.

more calories than are used by the body. Other factors increase the ease with which someone is able to become overweight or obese. Since the rise of consumerism and processed and convenience foods, people in the United States are marketed foods with lots of calories, fat, and sugar. Portion sizes have also increased. At the same time, it has become more difficult and more expensive to find and purchase whole foods such as vegetables and fruits.

Food scientists have begun looking into the connection between obesity and genetic makeup. Researchers have developed a thrifty genotype theory. These researchers hypothesize humans evolved to store energy as fat so they could survive times of scarcity. Now, with food available year-round in abundance, some argue the body's genes store more energy than is possible to use. But the thrifty gene may be only one of several fueling obesity. Others may cause people to overeat, tell the body to store more fat than is needed, or resist the need for physical activity. Future work in the genetics of obesity will help scientists understand the root causes of the disease.

Genetically Modified Organisms

Scientists, physicians, and environmental advocates are locked in a debate about the future of genetically altered seeds and foods. Genetically modified organism (GMO) technology was invented in the 1970s, and food

SEED PATENTS

Seed companies invest a lot of money and effort into the development of their GMO products. To protect their intellectual property, many companies file patents on the seeds they produce. Many companies require those who purchase seeds to sign an agreement that limits how the seeds can be used. For example, the seed company Monsanto sues farmers who collect seeds from plants grown from Monsanto seed. The company argues this policy helps ensure they are paid for their products and have the incentive to invest in research. The Supreme Court upheld the legality of Monsanto's policy in 2014. However, critics believe the patent policies go too far.

Some GMO opponents say the technology is too new to know the effects it will have on the environment and human health.

scientists started using it in the 1980s. They viewed it as the next innovation in the centuries-long history of manipulating foods to produce better products. One traditional example is selective breeding, or breeding for desired traits. Farmers often used only the seeds of plants that produced quality food, were disease-resistant, or had large yields. Similarly, ranchers selectively breed cattle for short legs and large trunks for the most meat possible.

Scientists are now able to alter the genetic makeup of foods to produce these desired traits. In the 1970s, researchers discovered a way to combine the DNA of two different organisms together. In 1983, scientists developed a process to increase production of these joined DNA strands so it was economically possible to produce GMOs. Food companies no longer had to rely on traditional methods to create foods with better traits. They could do it from the comfort of a laboratory. Food scientists started developing GMOs for commercial products, though their use was not approved by the FDA until the mid-1990s. Some of the first GMO products to be approved were soybeans, canola oil, rice, and corn. All of these foods are found in a wide variety of food products. According to the Grocery Manufacturers Association, 70 percent of all the food sold in US grocery stores in 2012 contained GMOs.[2]

Though GMOs have been beneficial for food companies, consumers and others are concerned about the lack of studies proving the safety of GMO foods. Environmentally, the main concern is the crossing of conventional crops with genetically modified ones in the field. This can pose food

HOW THE FDA EVALUATES GENETICALLY MODIFIED FOODS

The FDA has a process for evaluating and approving foods created from genetically modified plants. Food companies must work with the FDA throughout this process. First, a food company must identify whether its genetically modified plant could make a food toxic or cause allergies. The company must then compare the GMO with the conventional plant in regard to nutrition. It looks for protein, fat, fiber, and vitamin and mineral content. The FDA then reviews these findings and decides whether the GMO food can be sold.

safety and security risks. In the United States, for example, GMO corn that was only approved for animal feed crossbred with corn for human consumption.

Some people worry GMOs produced using the DNA of common allergens may pose a health risk. For example, companies may use nut DNA in a genetically modified soybean product. In the United States, companies do not need to label GMO foods as such. This means there is a potential for people with nut allergies to be exposed to nut DNA in a product containing soybeans. Another concern is known as gene transfer. Some scientists worry the genes that make some GMO foods resistant to antibiotics could be transferred to a person's gut bacteria.

Others, however, argue GMO foods have several advantages. They believe those who warn about the potential health and environmental risks of GMOs are using fear to dissuade people from eating these foods. The FDA asserts the genetically modified foods it has approved are safe for humans to eat. GMO supporters assert there may be advantages to developing GMOs, especially in the face of climate change. For example, plants can be engineered to be drought resistant. Food scientists continue to develop GMOs and research their effects on the environment and human health.

In 2010, 1 billion farmers across the world struggled to feed their families on the produce from two acres (0.8 ha) or fewer of land.[3] Drought, plant disease, and other unpredictable incidents can cause a crop to fail and families to starve. Fortunately, researchers at organizations across the globe are developing new technologies to

Western Seed Company's Saleem Esmail presents hybrid maize to Kofi Annan, chairman of Alliance for a Green Revolution in Africa.

FOODBORNE ILLNESS IN 2013

In 2013, the Centers for Disease Control investigated 11 multistate outbreaks of foodborne illness from both domestic and imported food products. Various strains of salmonella were responsible for five of the outbreaks, contaminating beef, chicken, cucumbers, and sesame paste. *E. coli* strains caused two outbreaks, one involving salad greens and another frozen food products. The other outbreaks were caused by vibrio parahaemolyticus and listeria, both bacteria; cyclospora, a parasite; and the Hepatitis A virus.[8]

make this type of small-scale farming more reliable. These technologies help farmers protect their crops from extreme weather and poor soil condition. Scientists have developed dozens of drought-resistant corn varieties. Jeff Raikes of the Bill & Melinda Gates Foundation believes 20 million farmers will be planting flood-resistant rice by 2017.[4]

The Global Table

It has become more and more common to cook a meal using ingredients from all across the world. It is now possible to go to the grocery store and purchase frozen catfish from China and blackberries from Guatemala and hundreds of other foods. In fact, 85 percent of the seafood available in the United States is imported.[5] But if not properly regulated, this global table can pose health risks, such as foodborne illness. In 2007, just 1.3 percent of all the foods imported to the United States were inspected by the FDA. Despite this, people in the United States eat approximately 260 pounds (118 kg) of imported food every year.[6]

Food imported to the United States is produced in 300,000 different factories in 150 countries.[7] This makes it incredibly difficult to regulate products coming into the United States. A 2012 study by the Centers for Disease Control revealed nearly 50 percent of all foodborne illness outbreaks in the United States involved imported foods. Fish were the most common source of illness, and 45 percent of the foods involved in outbreaks were imported from Asia.[9] Future food scientists will need to develop better ways to prevent and contain foodborne illness, while governments must look for ways to better inspect and regulate the foods that cross their borders.

The study of food science has been a global effort since people began to ponder food quality and develop ways to make food safer and more secure. As stated by Gratzer, "[The] history of nutritional science is full of fascination and drama, for it encompasses every virtue, defect, and [fault] of human nature."[10] The food scientists of tomorrow will continue to build on the innovations and discoveries of past scientists to uncover the remaining mysteries of nutrition, develop safer foods, and help ensure everyone has access to healthy foods.

Timeline

460 BCE Hippocrates develops the concept of the four humors.

160s Galen develops a nutritional theory based on Hippocrates's four humors.

1316 Europe experiences a famine, and approximately 10 percent of the continent's population dies.

1770 The region of Bengal, India, experiences a famine, killing approximately 10 million people.

1790s Nicolas Appert develops the first canning technique.

1798 Thomas Malthus publishes "Essay on the Principle of Population as it Affects the Future Improvement of Society."

1845–1855 The Irish Potato Famine kills more than 1 million people.

1855 Australian scientist James Harrison invents the first refrigeration system.

1860 Louis Pasteur's research on microorganisms leads to the invention of pasteurization.

1867 Justus von Liebig's Perfect Infant Food hits markets in England.

1869 Hippolyte Mège-Mouriès invents the first synthetic food, oleomargarine.

1896 Dutch physician Gerrit Grijns continues Christiaan Eijkman's beriberi research and discovers the existence of vitamins.

1906 The US Congress passes the Pure Food and Drug Act and the Federal Meat Inspection Act.

1915–1916 The "turnip winter" occurs in Germany during World War I.

1937 Joseph Goldberger's theory on the cause of pellagra is confirmed.

1943 The US federal government creates the first recommended daily allowances for food.

1957 Richard O. Marshall and Earl R. Kooi develop the process for making high-fructose corn syrup.

1973 The use of the insecticide DDT is banned in the United States.

1980 The FDA issues the pamphlet *Nutrition and Your Health: Dietary Guidelines for Americans* to help consumers make good food choices.

1994 The first Nutrition Facts labels appear on food packaging in the United States.

2014 The FDA proposes changes to update the Nutrition Facts labels.

Essential Facts

Canning

In the 1790s, Nicolas Appert discovered canning, a successful way of conserving foods using heat and glass jars. This method of preservation allowed food to last for much longer periods of time so it could then be transported to others in need, such as sailors or military personnel.

Genetically Modified Organisms (GMOs)

Food scientists invented GMO technology in the 1970s. While some are skeptical about the effects GMOs have on humans, the FDA assures they are approved for human consumption and can help increase and improve the food the world produces.

IMPACT ON SCIENCE

Throughout history, food science has helped scientists learn more about the role of food in our bodily functions, such as digestion. It has also helped scientists and nutritionists pinpoint the nutrition our bodies need, ways to use food to fight off foodborne illness, and ways to combat malnutrition, obesity, and starvation around the world.

Louis Pasteur

In 1860, Louis Pasteur conducted experiments in which he heated foods to 140 degrees Fahrenheit (60°C), in hopes of killing microorganisms in the food that made the food unhealthy for consumption. His method, now known as pasteurization, was successful in improving food preservation and safety and is still used today, such as the pasteurization of milk.

Christiaan Eijkman and Gerrit Grijns

In the 1890s, Christiaan Eijkman was tasked with discovering the cause of beriberi, a crippling disease. After injecting chickens with beriberi-infused blood and tampering with their white rice diet, his work concluded high starch levels increased the risk of beriberi. Gerrit Grijns further researched and built upon Eijkman's findings, concluding beriberi was a result of a vitamin B deficiency.

QUOTE

"[The] history of nutritional science is full of fascination and drama, for it encompasses every virtue, defect, and [fault] of human nature."

—Dr. Walter Gratzer, Terrors of the Table

Glossary

anatomy

The study of the structure of the human body.

anemia

A medical condition in which the body does not have enough red blood cells.

blockade

A barricade that prevents food and other goods from entering or leaving an area.

cholera

A serious infectious disease of the small intestine that causes diarrhea and vomiting.

commodity

A raw material that can be bought or sold, such as wheat or corn.

deficiency

A failing or shortcoming.

dysentery

An infection in the intestine that causes severe diarrhea.

famine

The very extreme scarcity of food.

food security

The state of having consistent access to affordable and nutritious food.

malnutrition

A condition that occurs when the body does not receive enough nutrients, especially from not having enough to eat or eating non-nutritious foods.

metabolism

The process the body uses to maintain life.

microorganism

An organism that can be seen only under a microscope.

parasite

An organism that needs to live in another organism in order to survive.

physiology

The study of the function of the parts of living organisms.

tuberculosis

An infectious disease that causes small lumps to grow in the lungs.

typhus

An infectious disease transmitted by lice, ticks, and fleas that causes fever, delirium, and death.

Additional Resources

Selected Bibliography

Collingham, Lizzie. *Taste of War: World War II and the Battle for Food*. New York: Penguin, 2011. Print.

Gratzer, Walter. *Terrors of the Table: The Curious History of Nutrition*. New York: Oxford UP, 2005. Print.

Lustig, Robert H. "What You Need to Know About Sugar." *Time*. Time, 27 Dec. 2012. Web. 13 June 2014.

Further Readings

Bartos, Judeen, ed. *Food Safety*. Detroit: Greenhaven, 2011. Print.

Forman, Lillian E. *Genetically Modified Foods*. Edina, MN: Abdo, 2010. Print.

Thornhill, Jan. *Who Wants Pizza? The Kids' Guide to the History, Science, and Culture of Food*. Toronto: Maple Tree, 2010. Print.

Websites

To learn more about History of Science, visit **booklinks.abdopublishing.com**. These links are routinely monitored and updated to provide the most current information available.

National Museum of American History

Fourteenth Street and Constitution Avenue, NW
Washington, DC, 20001
202-633-1000

http://americanhistory.si.edu/about/contact

The Smithsonian National Museum of American History's food collection encompasses the history of food in the United States, including canning equipment, advertising, and cook Julia Child's kitchen.

Penn State University Food Science Department

202 Rodney A. Erickson Food Science Building
University Park, PA 16802
814-865-5444

http://foodscience.psu.edu

The food science department at Penn State University is one of the best in the nation. Its students study food ingredients, food safety, manufacturing, and community food systems.

Source Notes

Chapter 1. Rickets, Putrid Meat, and Plumpy'Nut

1. "Achievements in Public Health, 1900-1999: Safer and Healthier Foods." *Morbidity and Mortality Weekly Report.* Centers for Disease Control, 15 Oct. 1999. Web. 13 May 2014.

2. Mary L. Bisland, ed. "Reforms Effected by Women." *The Illustrated American.* 6.53 (1891): 458. Print.

3. Ibid.

4. Jeffrey Heit. "Food Safety." *Medical Reference Guide.* University of Maryland Medical Center, 8 June 2012. Web. 15 May 2014.

Chapter 2. Ancient Theories to Renaissance Revelations

1. Michael C. Hickey. "I. Crisis." *The Late Middle Ages: Crisis and Recovers, 1300–1450.* Bloomsburg University of Pennsylvania, n.d. Web. 3 Jun. 2014.

Chapter 3. Birth of Modern Food Science

1. Vinita Damodaran. "Famine in Bengal: A Comparison of the 1770 Famine in Bengal and the 18907 Famine in Chotanagpur." *The Medieval History Journal.* 10 (2007): 143. Web. 11 May 2014.

2. Ibid.

3. Walter Gratzer. *Terrors of the Table: The Curious History of Nutrition.* New York: Oxford UP, 2005. Print. 120.

Chapter 4. Food Preservation and Safety

1. "Joseph Lister, Baron Lister." *Encyclopædia Britannica*. Encyclopædia Britannica, 2014. Web. 5 June 2014.

2. Uwe Kracht and Manfred Schulz, eds. *Food Security and Nutrition: The Global Challenge*. New York: St. Martin's, 1999. Print. 92.

3. "The Irish Potato Famine." *Digital History*. University of Houston, 13 May 2014. Web. 13 May 2014.

Chapter 5. The Government Gets Involved

1. Kenneth J. Carpenter. "The Nobel Prize and the Discovery of Vitamins." *Nobel Prize.org*. Nobel Media, 22 June 2004. Web. 13 May 2014.

2. Ibid.

3. United States Congressional House Committee on Agriculture. "Hearings Before the Committee on Agriculture on the So-Called 'Beveridge Amendment.'" *59th Congress, 1st Session*. Washington, DC: Government Printing Office, 1906. Print. 266.

4. "Celebrating 100 Years of FMIA." *USDA*. United States Department of Agriculture, n.d. Web. 14 May 2014.

Source Notes Continued

Chapter 6. Great War, Great Depression, Great Science

1. "World War I." *Encyclopædia Britannica*. Encyclopædia Britannica, 2014. Web. 5 June 2014.

2. Claire Suddath. "The Crash of 1929." *Time*. Time, 29 Oct. 2008. Web. 11 June 2014.

3. "Education Materials Index." *Army Heritage Center Foundation*. Army Heritage Center Foundation, n.d. 13 May 2014.

4. "Pellagra." *Medline Plus*. US National Library of Medicine, 14 Oct. 2012. Web. 13 May 2014.

5. Walter Gratzer. *Terrors of the Table: The Curious History of Nutrition*. New York: Oxford UP, 2005. Print. 112.

Chapter 7. The Rise of Agribusiness

1. Lizzie Collingham. *Taste of War: World War II and the Battle for Food*. New York: Penguin Press, 2012. Print. 1909.

2. Ibid. 1916.

3. D. Kromhout. "On the Waves of the Seven Countries Study." *ESC Lecture on Population Sciences*. European Heart Journal, 1999. Web. 13 June 2014.

4. "The Rise of American Consumerism." *American Experience*. PBS, n.d. Web. 27 May 2014.

Chapter 8. Emergence of the Food Label

1. Robert H. Lustig. "What You Need to Know About Sugar." *Time*. Time, 27 Dec. 2012. Web. 13 June 2014.

2. Sara Ipatenco. "How Much High-Fructose Corn Syrup Do We Consume?" *SFGate*. Hearst Communications, n.d. Web. 13 June 2014.

Chapter 9. The Future of Food Science

1. "The Obesity Epidemic." *CDC*. Centers for Disease Control, July 2011. Web. 15 June 2014.

2. Rachel Hennessey. "GMO Food Debate in the National Spotlight." *Forbes*. Forbes, 3 Nov. 2012. Web. 14 June 2014.

3. Michael J. Crumb. "World Food Conference Looks at Subsistence Farming." *Huffington Post*. TheHuffingtonPost.com, 13 Oct. 2010. Web. 15 June 2014.

4. Ibid.

5. Anna Edney. "Food Risk Rises as Import Reliance Makes US Safety Harder." *Bloomburg Businessweek*. Bloomburg, 4 Apr. 2012. Web. 15 June 2014.

6. Andrew Bridges. "Imported Food Rarely Inspected." *USA Today*. USA Today, 16 Apr. 2007. Web. 15 June 2014.

7. Anna Edney. "Food Risk Rises as Import Reliance Makes US Safety Harder." *Bloomburg Businessweek*. Bloomburg, 4 Apr. 2012. Web. 15 June 2014.

8. "List of Selected Outbreak Investigations by Year." *CDC*. Centers for Disease Control, 13 June 2014. Web. 16 June 2014.

9. "CDC Research Shows Outbreaks Linked to Imported Foods Increasing." *CDC*. Centers for Disease Control, 14 Mar. 2012. Web. 15 June 2014.

10. Walter Gratzer. *Terrors of the Table: The Curious History of Nutrition*. New York: Oxford UP, 2005. Print. vii.

Index

About the Author

Amanda Lanser is a freelance writer who lives in Minneapolis, Minnesota. She and her husband are animal lovers and have two cats, Quigley and Aveh, and a greyhound, Laila. Amanda enjoys writing books for kids of all ages and finds food history fascinating.

$$\frac{a+b}{a} = \frac{a}{b} = 1.618$$